Ethan's String

By: Tip Burwell

Printed in the United States of American
ISBN: 978-0-578-27020-3

Published by Ground Level Publishing
PO Box 2316
Hartsville, SC 29550
www.groundlevelpublishing.com

978-0-578-27020-3
Imprint: Ground Level Publishing

Dedication

I'd like to dedicate this book to my husband and three children. I've always wanted to write and publish a children's book about my own personal experiences, and now it's finally happened. Thank you all for the inspiration you've given to me from which I've been able to use in writing this book. I love you all!

It was just a simple string from the fringes of the throw blanket on the couch, but somehow it held Ethan's entire span of attention and entertainment.

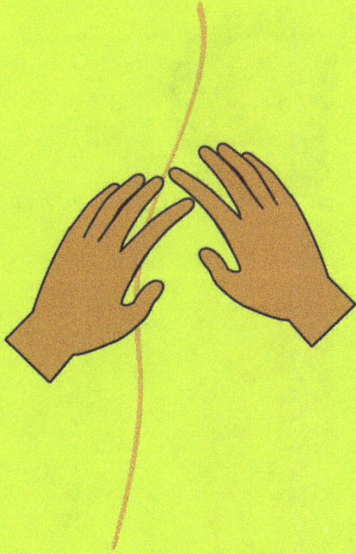

He held it between his
fingers as he shook his
hands with his free
fingers stretched out
taking turns to tap the
string, and Oh the
squeals; those happy,
high-pitched notes Ethan
would reach out of
sheer joy...

"I'm stimming. I like to stim," he'd say whenever Mom asked what he was doing. His smile would widen and Mom just looked at him lovingly and gently laughing, letting him know that it was okay and that she understood.

Ethan always said the cutest and funniest things.

Ethan is seven years old and he's (on the Autism Spectrum) autistic.

When he was two years old his parents noticed that he wasn't as engaged or as talkative as his two older siblings were at his age.

For example, Ethan was more fascinated by his left hand as he'd stare at it as if it was his friend. He'd wave it, shake it, hold it out in front of his face and just look at it all the time. This was called stimming from the word stimulating. These motions felt normal to Ethan.

Ethan's mom thought, "Well at least it's one string." She was remembering how Ethan once told her, "I could have thousands of strings," when looking at her throw blankets with fringes hanging. Although, Mom quickly told him, "But you only need one, so take good care of it." He agreed, and so here we are.

Ethan, so loving, so caring and hilarious. Mom would always tell people, "If "neurotypical" means normal with the way most kids act today, just selfish and self-absorbed, into all of their devices, hardly even wanting to talk to people, then I'll take my Ethan over that ANY day!"

Ethan loved to give hugs and kisses and was very social with people. He actually cared about how you were doing. It can be said that Ethan never met a stranger.

But dogs... dogs on the
other hand, not so much!
If Ethan saw a dog he'd
freeze up or panic.
Dogs were just too
unpredictable, after all.
You never knew if they
wanted to just sniff
you...or BITE you!!

Ethan had determined in his mind that he would not be taking any chances to find out which it would be. Of course he loved cartoon dogs, but he knew that they weren't really real, not like the dogs from the neighborhood. Ethan really did want to like dogs... until he saw one. But that's another story.

However, with his string, Ethan would hold it when he ate, when he played, when he brushed his teeth, but never when he bathed. He didn't want it to get wet after all.. But it was the first thing he'd grab once he dried off.

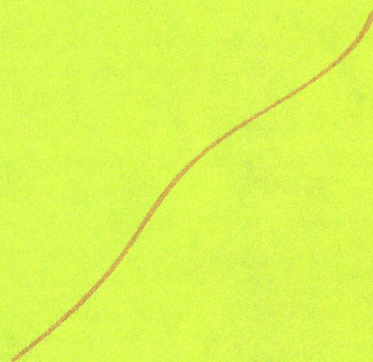

"Hand it over," his big brother would command. "Ethan, you're too old to play with strings," his sister would insist. "Do you want people to make fun of you...?" Ethan would just say, "But I like playing with my string because I like to stim."

That was Ethan's story and he was sticking to it. But on this particular day, Ethan had lost his string...again. So, this was a problem for EVERYBODY! Especially for his mother, or should we say her throw blankets on the couches.

They had lots of fringes hanging from them, lots of different colors too, which made for a plentiful stock pile of strings for Ethan. If he'd lose one well there were plenty more where that came from. Mom's throw blankets were almost literally hanging on by a thread.

Ethan was on a search. He searched his bed; sometimes he would put his string under his pillow, but it was not there.

Then he went into the den, the living room, his sister's room, his brother's room, his parent's room searching on the floor on all fours bending, stretching, wanting so desperately to find his favorite string, but it was no where to be found.

He looked under the bed, around the bed, under his rug, but it wasn't there either.

"Well maybe you don't need your string. Maybe your string found a new home", Mom replied. "You know you're getting to be a big boy now and maybe you're getting too old to play with strings." Ethan's face fell. He looked sadly and deeply at his mother and slowly said.,"Yes, I guess you're... right."

Then he let out a long sigh. His eyes began to fill with tears as he then blurted out, "But I want my string!" Then Ethan ran to his room. Immediately, Mom felt sorry for suggesting this. She knew how much the string meant to Ethan and besides, who was it really bothering anyway?

Then, it slowly occurred to Mom about how most everybody constantly have their hands fidgeting with something and have their own habits, just like Ethan. Why, she had them too. And didn't her other two children have some kind of a habit when they were Ethan's age, too? Of course. Whether it was slime, a yo-yo, silly putty, or a fidget spinner...

After all, how much of snapping fingers, squeezing stress balls, and yes even using apps on cell phones ways to keep people's hands moving or occupied? It was now so clear and Mom knew exactly what needed to be done. She collected the items and then went to Ethan's door and knocked. "May I come in?"

A sniffle, then a sigh came from the other side. Then, "Yes ma'am"... Mom walked in and sat down on Ethan's bed. He was looking at her with big eyes, awaiting the apology he knew was coming. Mom would give him big hugs when she wanted him to feel better.

But this time instead of just a hug, Mom presented Ethan with lots of strings in lots of different colors.

They were extra long and clearly from her blankets. Ethan was so surprised. He slowly reached for them and after realizing that now Mom understood, and that it was okay for him to use them to stim, Ethan reached up and grabbed his Mom's waist, giving her the biggest hug ever.

Mom was certain that it was each and every day that Ethan pulled on strings, the heartstrings! He wasn't "atypical", but rather a typical kid, unique in his own way.

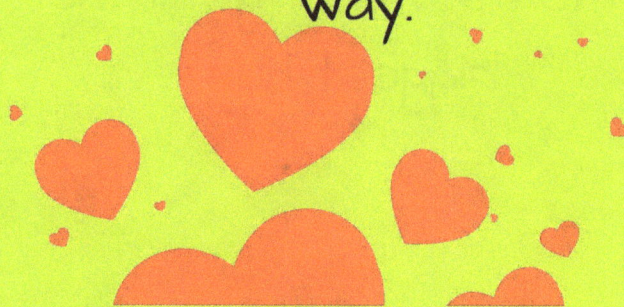

About the Author

Tip Burwell is a mother of an autistic child. She is passionate about spreading truth and awareness and is an advocate for her son, of whom this book is written. With a Bachelors of Science degree in Communications/Media Production from East Carolina University, she uses her background to produce content that is engaging and relatable that will hopefully lead to a greater understanding and appreciation for people from all walks of life.